Helen of Troy is High AF

Sonia Greenfield

Harbor Editions
Small Harbor Publishing

Helen of Troy is High AF
Copyright © 2023 SONIA GREENFIELD
All rights reserved.

Cover art "Without Sanctuary" by Jen Stein Hauptmann
Cover design by Allison Blevins
Book layout by Allison Blevins and Hannah Martin

HELEN OF TROY IS HIGH AF
SONIA GREENFIELD
ISBN 978-1-957248-08-0
Harbor Editions,
an imprint of Small Harbor Publishing

Contents

Invocation / **9**

Penelope Tries to Invoke the Inverse / **11**

Athena Understands the Limitations
    of Her Power / **13**

Scylla and Charybdis Speak: A Poem
    for Two Voices / **15**

Zeus's Eagles Explain Themselves / **17**

Helen of Troy is High AF / **18**

Ino, the White Goddess, as Caregiver / **21**

The Concubines of Cicones / **23**

Nausicaa Dresses Odysseus / **24**

Arete Understands Her Place / **26**

Circe in the Age of Instagram / **27**

Calypso Keeps What She Finds / **29**

Anticleia and Eurycleia Speaking to Odysseus: A Poem
    for Two Voices / **31**

Siren Song / **33**

Melantho Does Melantho / **35**

A Servant in the House of Odysseus Confesses Prior
    to Her Hanging / **36**

Helen of Troy is High AF

Someone will remember us, I say; even in another time.
—Sappho

Invocation

Muse, do not tell me
of a Janus-faced man,

but instead come
unbound by convention,

unwind yourself
from the lengths

men go to dress rage
as glory, and drop

your toga of time
to the floor. Muse,

do not tell me
of his trials. Do not

speak of his hands
covered in the slick

gore of murder.
Muse, do not tire

me with appeals
to pity. Do not play

your plaintive strains
meant to make me weep

for poor Odysseus.
Muse, it's time

to bring forward
the whispers—

it's time to let
women speak.

Penelope Tried to Invoke the Inverse

It's possible to desire the marble
hard torso of a spouse and still

despise the sex. That is, the gender
draped on every surface of this palace

with appetites as ravenous as Scylla.
I am the very model of ambivalence.

You ask, *Could I cut a throat?* I could,
but I am always outnumbered. Can you

imagine it the other way around? Put me
to bed on an island so I can miss my son

even as I admit he is but one more
blackhole sucking all energy

to his center. Let me take Calypso
as a lover and leave Odysseus here

to entertain a hall full of flirts simpering
each morning at their mirrors and weaving

my best ribbons through their hair.
Let Sappho write it since Homer has

no taste for the homoerotic. His stories
always slanted to uphold the glories of men—

that slick way he writes his own fetish
into the record. Imagine each morning

his lord ignoring the arching backs
and curves of each girl asleep

a floor below. Imagine him keeping chaste
a decade while his whole home hums

with lust as loud as a clover field of bees.
You can't, can you? Even I must admit

how a good man might partition loyalty
from what hunger wakes him every day,

while a woman, one-minded,
can keep busy at her loom.

Athena Understands the Limitations of Her Power

I can be the Goddess of Wisdom,
Goddess of Warfare, Goddess

of Freedom, gray-eyed Goddess
of Levelheadedness and protector

of Athens; I can lead heroes home
from battle, summon a whole air

fleet of owls to destroy rival
armies, save Perseus, Heracles,

Bellerophon, and Jason even while
stirring up the Trojan War. I can

weave warmth from tapestries of ice,
turn a competitor to spider

and for her own good a rape victim
into Gorgon. Worshippers will spill

the blood of their best bulls in my honor
and build temples to earn my favor

or practice physical prowess at festivals
feting me, Goddess of almost anything,

but we all know I assumed the guise
of Mentor to gird Telemachus, one more

boy who would never buy what sage words
a woman offered, like they were spoken

from her very slit. Even on Olympus,
I am Athena, Goddess of sword and shield

and common sense, yet still I simper
at my father's knee: always daddy's little girl

scrambling to be heard over the drone
of Godly baritones bending his ear.

Scylla and Charybdis Speak:
A Poem for Two Voices

As if we're allowed to speak
in anything but a teeth-shattering

screech of yearning. *As if we make
any noise but for a constant sucking*

sound. Man or Zeus could devour
every fish in the sea. *But God forbid*

*a nymph should want more than
her share.* Traverse the slim path

between the hollowness that roils
my gut *and the depth of my starvation.*

We are built of longing; *we are
made of nothing but desire.* This is

what want looks like: sun-bleached
garden of bones and my every head

picking clean each sinew of sailor.
This is what nearly sated screams like:

*to eat and eat every ship's beam delivered
to the floor of the Aegean where I am*

chained. Don't you recognize our
guise? *This eternal curse for daring*

to hunger? Every woman knows
we're supposed to be thankful

for scraps. *Every woman
knows we were meant to be empty.*

Zeus's Eagles Explain Themselves

We were commanded, yes, and given
talons to claw into the soft sides

of morsels—mammal
and fledgling—even making meals

of the muscular ropiness of reptiles;
given a hooked beak to spring open

the skin of any unlucky beast small
enough to make quick work of—

skin unpeeled to the prized pulse
of blood beneath—we make ribbons

of meat and entrails to swallow whole.
It was asked of us, yes, to take these

weapons of meal-making to the faces
of suitors who bully and mock, who make

a game of shoving the weak even with
words and sleep best with dreams

drenched incarnadine by carnage.
Requested, yes, but we ask: *Wouldn't*

you want to rip into, claws honed
vicious, the casual cruelty of these men?

Helen of Troy is High AF

> *Then the child of Zeus, Helen, decided she would mix the wine with drugs to take all pain and rage away, to bring forgetfulness of every evil.*
> —Book 4, *The Odyssey*

If I knew the difference
between entomology

and etymology, I'd know
my either; I'd know if you meant

meaning or just a clacking
of beetles, just a phalanx

of carapace carried
by a hundred legs as in *centi*

or thousand as in *milli*, but my mind
is modest these days. Even

modestly minded I know
it's no mistake that abduction

shares a word with what
penetrates me: *rape*. What do

you know from one? Was she
merely hogtied and dragged

in a flaxen bag from all
she ever knew or was she

pressed face to the dirt and
entered? Either way, they say

rape. If you wonder what made
this face, this curve of cheek,

consider how candlelight catches
faint down where my jaw

meets this elegance of neck.
You must recall my mother

was force fucked by a swan.
That's our fate. Our citizenship

so tenuous we are even taken
by birds. You've heard how

we bury our children, how we watch
war made with wooden horses,

how we are dragged to hell because
poor Hades needs a date.

As consolation they give us
poppy powder for our wine. I say

another dram of dream in mine.
I am such a scholar for forgetting,

such a student for letting go. I say
set the table to a swarm of servants

buzzing in the corners of this
opulent palace. I say anoint

the chalice to Menelaus who
lets me be as shitfaced as I please

until morning wipes the prior day
clean, and I can try living again.

Until then, I may hallucinate
that the thousand launched ships

never come back. Will you,
my guest, drink to that?

Ino, The White Goddess, as Caregiver

If I am the caps of froth
that waves wear

and doff in calm
conditions, in encountering

Odysseus, you wonder
why I lift him up.

Wine-dark, the silver
underpinning water

all but poisoned by
salt, the sea churns me

as if I were borne along
by fingertips prodding

all my soft spaces. I do
what I can, though sailors

will blame and name
anything *She* like we

have it out for them.
Like they never see

when I bear them to safety,
when their maiden ships

nurture them to harbor.
I encountered Odysseus

who was drowning,
and what woman would

hang back and let
her heart beat wild

while watching him
sink? We think we can

save every man
from himself.

The Concubines of Cicones

> *We took their wives and shared their riches equally among us.*
> —Book 9, *The Odyssey*

Concubine is a pretty word,
like *clementine*, like *serpentine*,

like *gossamer*, like *chauffer*,
like *aurora*, like *plethora*,

like *petrichor*, like *epicure*,
like *serendipity*, like *exquisitely*,

like *solitude*, like *maroon*,
like *supine*, like *sublime*,

like *pluvial*, like *marsupial*,
like *euphemism*, like what words

can do when meant to
obscure meaning, overlaid

like hot breath huffed
ragged in your ear.

Nausicaa Dresses Odysseus

A princess, and yet, sent to the beach
to do laundry, so we scrubbed a kingdom's

worth of robes. What to do with women's
work but make a game of it, to play when

the elder men weren't staring stern
and saying you are to be seen and not

heard, like children, as if we were merely
trifles to be admired? Imagine, then,

a naked man emerging from behind
a shrub. You can, can't you? Just one

of many exposures, I'm sure. There's
something in a brute that loves to foist

his phallus upon the world, so it was hard
to believe he had no intention to shock

with his body, to use his cock as a cudgel
meant to beat our innocence senseless.

But no. He hadn't a stitch of clothes,
an apparent castaway washed to shore,

though there was something alpha
in the way his body was built by its

simmering barbarity. Still, we tossed him
tunic and fustanella to cover in order

to prostrate before king and queen, and I
came to find him almost irresistible, even if

he was old like Zeus himself. I might say
it was how he didn't want to offend,

or how he hoisted his little flag of honor
for a shoreline of washerwomen, or just

that he wasn't wholly repulsive, but I
have come to recognize in my young years

how, for mate or fate, for what befalls
or uplifts, even for what might grow

into love, a woman must
manage her expectations.

Arete Understands Her Place

Here is the hearth of my husband, the son
of my husband, the daughter of my husband,

the subjects of my husband, and the goodwill
of my husband who leans hard into what I bring

to our union: youth, as I am a third his age; beauty—
if I am a wealth of good angles, he is but a pauper;

and smarts, yet only behind closed doors do I dare
outwit him in the little games we play to keep

our minds supple. I can't help but thank the Gods
every day for how he dotes on me and lets out

my reins enough to pretend equal power.
I conduct a household like a symphony

that plays the floors gleaming, that ignites
all the lamps and sets a goblet before the master

home once again from a long week of sacking.
Every night to the mirror I beg gray-eyed Athena

to smooth the furrow cut into my brow,
and every night, out of sympathy, she gathers

all the errant lines of my face in her fist and, like
a magic trick, shakes them into straw

distributed to her owls who line their nests
with every woman's almost obsolescence.

Circe in the Age of Instagram

*Nothing is anachronism
if you live forever*, it says

in my bio. I started with
carefully composed shots

of the island, sun filtered
through olive grove and arbor,

close-ups of hermit crabs
hurrying their little conches

across the sand. Every
influencer knows what we

go through to make labor
look like love. Twenty takes

trying to get that thirst trap.
Gently slopping the hogs,

hair curled by afternoon
heat, gorgeous in torn coveralls

with my bright red bucket.
Post it. How else to turn

vengeance to magic and magic
to commerce? Sometimes

we're even the beneficiaries
of serendipity, sun somehow

netted behind a new sail
arriving on shore, shot

perfectly composed, as the next
set of sailors straggle into

foreground. I post it. A girl
must make the best

of what she possesses. I share
daily stories of how they squirm

and tumble over each other,
adorable montages of snouts

snuffing the lens. I filter
the ugly out of muddy

trotters and mottled skin,
I give them stupid names like

Pigasus and Hogamemnon—
then satisfy every order:

belly, shoulder,
bacon, and loin.

Calypso Keeps What She Finds

*His eyes were always tearful; he wept sweet life away, in
longing to go back home, since she no longer pleased him.*
—Book 5, *The Odyssey*

Imagine a man washing up
on your land like driftwood

and worn by waves
to the very shape you crave.

Imagine being able to shrug
off the mantle of time as if

it were a loose-woven
cloak of wool, but saying

no; saying you'd rather go.
Yes, I kept what I found,

and he kept me always
undressed in a cave

that stored in every crevice
the sound of surf. I kept him

in wine and cypress smoke,
kept him clipped nearly wingless

on an isle of birds. What of it?
Let me tell you something

of wetness, my land slick in even
its sacred spaces, and also what

fickle means. He fucked me good
for seven years until nostalgia

sparkled like something new again.
Let him shove off from shore

and be tossed toward home.
I have no more patience

for a man fooled into mistaking
each morning's horizon line

for something novel, no patience
for a man hot on the heels

of Helios, happy to chase
each day to its close.

Anticleia and Eurycleia Speaking to Odysseus: A Poem for Two Voices

If I am the mother who birthed you, *then I
am the mother who raised you, who nursed you.* Imagine

a connection as tenuous as spider silk,
unwombed, and then passing you in a hall

swaddled in her arms, *as I lead you to suckle.*
In the underworld where I landed after falling

through dirt as fine as clouds, you finally
come as one more son in the omnipresent

and ancient history of those who never
call their mothers; *in the omnipresent and ancient*

*history of sons threatening violence against their mothers,
you would cut my throat were I to reveal you to your wife*

and her suitors. If I have slipped away from you
back into the soup of hell, it is only because you

forsook me first, for bloodlust, as men do to
their mothers who must make loaves of mourning

then eat them every day. *If I have recognized you,
it is by one of the scars you wear like merit badges*

*awarded for violent efforts, this time against animals driven
to gore.* Who soothed you with salve and wrapped

your wound? *Was it she who soothed you with salve,
wrapped your wound, then made a meal of the foul boar?*

Odysseus, why do boys distain those who would
sever their own veins and feed them into the mouths

of selfsame boys who would siphon us dry? *Odysseus,
why do sons assume us stupid enough to spill their secrets?*

Siren Song

We sing for ourselves
and in sorority harmonize

sounds that drown
sailors. We did not

invite them to this rock
where we prefer our own

company, where we comb
little crabs from each other's

hair or make crafts with
the flotsam of their

arrogance. We do not ask
them to call on us, to fall

from the decks of ships
into the churn—whirling

waves we thought we put
between them and us.

We specifically fled
to mists where nymphs

go to get away from
their pleading and those

catchy songs requesting
our yield so they can

slurp us like oysters
sucked from their shells.

Melantho Does Melantho

Say you spent your girlhood among
the goat herd, collecting milk in your bucket

or brushing coarse hair with a stiff brush.
Say you grew accustomed to the gamey smell

of the yard, flies drunk on the funk of
dung, the way the herd ate everything

down to dirt. Say you loved the hourglass
of their eyes, how they butted against your

leg for a scratch or distained with a bleat
when penned for the night. Say, too,

you thought yourself indispensable
as the young do until mature enough for

market. Say you were sold by your parents for
the certainty of food, even as your brother

remained free, even if you were the one the nannies
loved, the one they let their kids be led by

to slaughter. Say something feral simmered
under your skin as you supplicated at the knee

of Penelope, though you were her favorite,
the one she gave little gifts to, as if any bauble

were as precious as sovereignty. You call
my actions acts of betrayal. I say opportunity.

A Servant in the House of Odysseus Confesses Prior to Her Hanging

> *. . . he wound a piece of sailor's rope round the rotunda and round the mighty pillar, stretched up so high no foot could touch the ground.*
> —Book 22, *The Odyssey*

The conquering is like waves
that break and break again against

the shores of Ithaca until every ounce
of humanity is washed away. First, it's

the man, then it's the land, then all
of the fallen women corralled

and distributed among favored
houses at the whim of what power

creates when it fluctuates between
forces and their pitiful pissing

contests. I am a cat on a string;
I am a kite on a string—I am no

thing but what the masters make
of me, taken at twelve from Troy

and taught to pleasure soldiers
lucky enough to be Athena's

pet project, but who protects
me? To the gods we are

nothing but the sound of static
in their ears, our cries heard like

tinnitus only when their halls fall
silent. You say I betrayed, that I laid

with men set to unseat Odysseus
from his throne, but that implies

free will. I have had none.
I am done and to be strung

as an ornament in the winds
that have always blown against me,

all my protestations strangled
to silence until I can cross that river

and sit with my mother again,
where I can braid her hair still caked

with the gore of stuck suitors,
and we can be liberated finally from

the bodies that ferried us
through this terrible ordeal.

Acknowledgments and Notes

"Scylla and Charybdis Speak: A Poem for Two Voices" first appeared in *Copper Nickel*.

"Helen of Troy is High AF" first appeared in *Ample Remains*.

"Calypso Keeps What She Finds" first appeared in the *Los Angeles Review*.

"Circe in the Age of Instagram" first appeared in *On the Seawall*.

All epigraphs from The Odyssey were taken from the Emily Wilson translation (W.W. Norton, 2018).

Sonia Greenfield (she/they) is the author of *All Possible Histories* (Riot in Your Throat, 2022), *Letdown* (White Pine Press, 2020), *American Parable* (Autumn House, 2018), and *Boy with a Halo at the Farmer's Market* (Codhill Press, 2015). Her work has appeared in the 2018 and 2010 *Best American Poetry, Southern Review, Willow Springs,* and elsewhere. She lives with her family in Minneapolis where she teaches at Normandale College, edits the *Rise Up Review,* and advocates for both neurodiversity and the decentering of the cis/het white hegemony. You can find more at soniagreenfield.com.

www.ingramcontent.com/pod-product-compliance
Lightning Source LLC
Chambersburg PA
CBHW051705040426
42446CB00009B/1310